WOMEN PROFILE

WOMEN ROLE IN BIBLE

M. PRABHU TEJA

Copyright © M. Prabhu Teja
All Rights Reserved.

Contents

Foreword

"Nevertheless, in the Lord woman is not independent of man nor man of woman; for as woman was made from man, so man is now born of woman. And all things are from God." 1 Corinthians 11-12

It's easy for the Bible to overpower your memory with all the stories of powerful men. However, there are stories of equally strong females. God created women with intention. Throughout the Bible, there are many women that showcase that intention.

This book will showcase some of the amazing females of Christianity. These important women in the Bible served crucial roles in furthering God's word. and encourages you to run a powerful ministry.

Preface

The role of women in ministry tends to be a controversial topic. So, I'll preface my thoughts by saying this: Whether you come from an egalitarian viewpoint (men's and women's roles are equal in every way, including serving as elders, preachers, etc.) or a complementarian outlook (men's and women's roles are different, but they complement one another for the glory of God), I anticipate you will agree with the thoughts I share in this book. I also said here what is the role of women in bible and their roles in church.

I strongly encourage all Christians to know the Bible, and this book showed why that's so important among Christian women. In "Commitment to Family, Faith, Career & Community: Mothers Juggle It All,". "Moms are [children's] foremost partners in prayer (63 percent) and conversations about God (70 percent), the Bible (71 percent), or other faith questions (72 percent). The years that show mothers are the managers of faith formation (among other household routines and structures)." Additionally, women tend to compete for attention among the many distractions going on around us, which makes it even more important that women consciously take time to learn about God and spend time with him. "Look to the Lord and his strength; seek his face always" (1 Chronicles 16:11).

Introduction

There are many voices in the world today speaking on behalf of women.

-We have heard the voice of what has been termed in some nations "women's liberation" calling for equal rights for all women everywhere.

-In other nations, the voice of tradition has been raised demanding that women be kept in subjection.

-Theologians have debated extensively regarding the role of women in the Church.

-We have heard the voices of psychologists, educators, and philosophers with their various views on womanhood.

In general, concern with the subject of women has focused on their purpose and position in society. Many modern movements promoting liberation for women have overreacted to the problems and concerns faced by women.

The movement towards liberation for women is not new. It can be traced back to the first woman, Eve, who sought liberation from God's rules. But true liberation for women comes only through Jesus Christ and recognition of the patterns and principles governing womanhood revealed in God's Word, the Bible.This course summarizes allthe Bible teaches regarding women.

It is not only a study guide, but a reference tool as it lists all the passages about women and references to all the individual women mentioned in the Word of God. Now, "Let the earth hear His voice" on the subject of womanhood as we develop from Scripture.

CHAPTER ONE

In The Beginning

INTRODUCTION The book of Genesis in the Holy Bible is referred to as the book of beginnings. It records the beginning of the world, of man and woman, of sin and God's plan for salvation, and the formation of the nations. The first chapter of Genesis describes the creation of the world. The second chapter tells of the creation of man with a reference to woman in 1:27.

The main references describing the origin of woman are Genesis chapter 2 Genesis 2 concludes the description of God's week of creation and then zooms in on the creation of man, his work, his perfect environment, and the creation of woman as his helper and wife. It is our last glimpse of the world before it is ravaged by human sin and death with the disobedience of Adam and Eve in chapter 3.

Where chapter 1 gave a full overview of creation, this chapter focuses more on a few specific events. These are crucial to understanding the fall of man. Bible reveals that women was created by God Genesis 2:7 states that man was created by God from the dust of the earth. God breathed into man the breath of life, and he became a living soul.

God decided it was not good for Adam to be alone (Genesis 2:22).

God caused a deep sleep to fall on Adam, then He took one of his ribs and from it created the first woman who was named Eve.Adam called his mate woman, which means "she-man" or "joined to man," because she was taken out of man. This is where the word "woman" originated.

GOD CREATED IN HIS IMAGE:

(Genesis 2:26-27) documents that God created both male and female in His image: "And God said, Let us make man in our image, after our likeness...So God created man in His own image, in the image of God created He him; male and female created He them". (Genesis 1:26-27). God's First responsibility to Man God gives four instructions: Be fruitful (or "bear fruit," have babies). Multiply (as each new generation has more kids and they have more kids). Fill the earth (populate). Have dominion (or authority and management) over all the other creatures.

These commands frame many important aspects of a Christian worldview. One crucial point to note is that the commands to reproduce and multiply came prior to the fall of man in Genesis chapter 3. In blunt terms, this means that God created mankind with the capacity for sex, and sexual reproduction, and intended us to utilize those abilities. Sex, therefore, is not sinful in and of itself.

Of course, like all good things, sex has a proper context: marriage. And yet, this simple point—that God created us as intentionally sexual creatures—speaks against the recurring myth that the Bible considers sex itself to be morally wrong. As explained in Genesis chapter 2, God would directly create only two humans. The rest of us would come from them, one generation after the next. Humankind's first responsibilities would be to fill up the earth with people and to care for the earth as God's representatives.

WOMAN'S RELATIONSHIP TO GOD

Woman was created by God, in the image of God, with an eternal soul (Genesis 2:7) related to God in a special union. This relationship is spiritual because God is a spirit (John 4:24). God enjoyed a spiritual relationship with Adam and Eve (Genesis 3:8). This union was broken due to man's fall into sin, but God provided a plan to restore man's spiritual relationship with his Creator.

The relationship of woman to man was one of:

LOVE: The creation of woman from man is an example of the type of relationship that would later exist between Jesus Christ and the Church. While Adam slept, his side was opened and woman was created. Centuries later when Jesus Christ hung on the cross for the sins of all mankind, through the great sleep of His death the Church was created.

Christ's side was pierced with a spear and there came forth a creative flow of blood to redeem and water to purify the Church. 'Husbands, love your wives, just as Christ loved the church and gave himself up for her.' 'to make her holy, cleansing her by the washing with water through the word', (Ephesians 5:25-26). The creation of woman speaks of a love relationship, similar to that which exists between Christ and the Church. This is a deep, enduring, spiritual love, not a sensual relationship based on external charm or beauty. God said He would create a "help meet" for man (Genesis 2:18).

The same Hebrew word for help meet, Azyer, occurs forty times in the Old Testament and is often used to speak of God as helper of His people. The word does not mean subjection, as God is certainly not subject to man. Rather, it pictures a giving, loving, caring, relationship of help similar to that which exists between God and man. Genesis 2:24 speaks of the relationship of commitment between man and woman.

The man is to : Leave his father and mother: Mental commitment.

Cleave unto his wife: Emotional commitment

They shall be one flesh: Physical commitment.

Love, companionship, commitment, and a mutual helping relationship are qualities of the union God designed between man and woman.

CHAPTER TWO

THE FALL OF WOMEN

Now the serpent was more crafty than any other wild animal that the Lord God had made. He said to the woman, "Did God say, 'You shall not eat from any tree in the garden'?" The woman said to the serpent, "We may eat of the fruit of the trees in the garden; but God said, 'You shall not eat of the fruit of the tree that is in the middle of the garden, nor shall you touch it, or you shall die.' " But the serpent said to the woman, "You will not die; for God knows that when you eat of it your eyes will be opened, and you will be like God, knowing good and evil." So when the woman saw that the tree was good for food, and that it was a delight to the eyes, and that the tree was to be desired to make one wise, she took of its fruit and ate; and she also gave some to her husband, who was with her, and he ate.

The serpent's plan succeeds, and first Eve, then Adam, eats the fruit of the forbidden tree. They break the limits God had set for them, in a vain attempt to become "like God" in some way beyond what they already had as God's image-bearers (Gen. 3:5). Already knowing from experience the goodness of God's creation, they choose to become "wise" in the ways of evil (Gen. 3:4-6). Eve's and Adam's decisions to eat the fruit are choices to favor their own pragmatic, aesthetic, and sensual tastes over God's word. "Good" is no longer rooted in what God says enhances life but in what people think is desirable to elevate life. In short, they turn what is good into evil.

By choosing to disobey God, they break the relationships inherent in their own being. First, their relationship together—"bone of my bones and flesh of my flesh," as it had previously been (Gen. 2:23)—is driven apart as they hide from each other under the cover of fig leaves (Gen. 3:7). Next to go is their relationship with God, as they no longer talk with him in the evening breeze, but hide themselves from his presence (Gen. 3:8). Adam further breaks the relationship between himself and Eve by blaming her for his decision to eat the fruit, and getting in a dig at God at the same time. "The woman whom you gave to be with me, she gave me fruit from the tree, and I ate" (Gen. 3:12). Eve likewise breaks humanity's relationship with the creatures of the earth by blaming the serpent for her own decision (Gen. 3:13).

Adam's and Eve's decisions that day had disastrous results that stretch all the way to the modern workplace. God speaks judgment against their sin and declares consequences that result in difficult toil. The serpent will have to crawl on its belly all its days (Gen. 3:14). The woman will face hard labor in delivering children, and also feel conflict over her desire for the man (Gen. 3:16).

The man will have to toil to wrest a living from the soil, and it will produce "thorns and thistles" at the expense of the desired grain (Gen. 3:17-18). All in all, human beings will still do the work they were created to do, and God will still provide for their needs (Gen. 3:17-19). But work will become more difficult, unpleasant, and liable to failure and unintended consequences. It is important to note that when work became toil, it was not the beginning of work. Some people see the curse as the origin of work, but Adam and Eve had already worked the garden.

Work is not inherently a curse, but the curse affects the work. In fact, work becomes more important as a result of the Fall, not less, because more work is required now to yield the necessary results. Furthermore, the source materials from which Adam and Eve sprang in God's freedom and pleasure now become sources of subjugation. Adam, made from dirt, will now struggle to till the soil until his body returns to dirt at his death (Gen. 3:19); Eve, made from a rib in Adam's side, will now be subject to Adam's domination, rather than taking her place beside him (Gen. 3:16).

Domination of one person over another in marriage and work was not part of God's original plan, but sinful people made it a new way of relating when they broke the relationships that God had given them (Gen. 3:12-13). Two forms of evil confront us daily. The first is natural evil, the physical conditions on earth that are hostile to the life God intends for us. Floods and droughts, earthquakes, tsunamis, excessive heat and cold, disease, vermin, and the like cause harm that was absent from the garden.

The second is moral evil, when people act with wills that are hostile to God's intentions. By acting in evil ways, we mar the creation and distance ourselves from God, and we mar the relationships we have with other people. We live in a fallen, broken world and we cannot expect life without toil. We were made for work, but in this life that work is stained by all that was broken that day in the Garden of Eden. This too is often the result of failing to respect the limits God sets for our relationships, whether personal, corporate, or social.

The Fall created alienation between people and God, among people, and between people and the earth that was to support them. Suspicion of one another replaced trust and love. In the generations that followed, alienation nourished jealousy, rage, even murder. All workplaces today reflect that alienation between workers—to greater or lesser extent—making our work even more toilsome and less productive.

PENALTIES FOR SIN

• Changed physical form: The physical form Satan used for the temptation was cursed. 21The serpent, or snake, originally walked upright but from this time on wiggled on his belly through the dust.

• Enmity between Satan and man: This was the beginning of what we call "spiritual warfare," with Satan struggling for the soul of man. This warfare continues to the present day. Harvestime International Institute offers a course entitled "Spiritual Strategies" which focuses on this spiritual warfare and provides strategies for victory over the enemy.

• A crushed head: The third penalty on the serpent is actually a promise to sinful man. Although Satan would "bruise the heel" of man spiritually through sin, the seed (descendant) that would come from woman would crush the head of Satan (Genesis 3:15). This was the first promise of a Savior for the sin of mankind. Although Satan would affect man through sin, a Savior would be sent by God through woman and the power of sin would be crushed. The tragedy of sin came through the fall of one woman, but redemption would also come through a woman who would birth the Lord Jesus Christ.

- ON ADAM :

Labor a weariness: Prior to sin Adam tended the ground in happiness, but now he must labor hard. The environment of the earth changed. The ground that was once fertile and without pests or weeds became filled with thorns and thistles.

Death: The penalty of natural death was imposed on Adam. God said his body would return to the ground, for "dust thou art, and unto dust shalt thou return." Spiritual death was also a penalty of sin. God said "the soul that sinneth, it shall die" (Ezekiel 18:20). Without forgiveness, man would die the spiritual death of eternal separation from God

- ON EVE:

Sorrow in childbirth: The curse of pain and sorrow was placed upon child bearing. Subjection: Eve would become subject to her husband. (We will deal more with the concept of submission later in this course as we study the Epistles)..

The Beginning and The end : In these first two chapters we known about the events which occurred when the first woman was created. The book of Revelation provides interesting contrasts between the beginning and end. Read Revelation chapters 21 and 22 which describe the final days of time and the new heaven and earth God has planned for His people

Genesis

- Paradise closed 3:23
- Dispossesion through sin 3:24
- Curse imposed 3:17
- Access to tree denied 3:24

- Beginning of sorrow, death 3:16-19
- Garden defiled 3:5-7
- Man's dominion broken 3:19.
- Evil triumphs 3:13
- Walk of God with man interrupted 3:8-10

Revelation

- Paradise opened 21:25
- Repossession through grace 21:24
- Curse removed 22:3
- Access permitted 22:14
- Ending of sorrow, death 21:4
- No defilement 21:27
- Dominion restored 21:5
- Good triumphs 21:10
- Relationship resumed 21:3

Although the fall into sin was a sad moment in history, the future for all mankind is one of joyful anticipation through Jesus Christ.

CHAPTER THREE

WOMEN FAITH IN THE BIBLE

God's Word speaks very highly of those who had faith. There are many examples of women of faith in the Bible, and we can know much by studying their stories. Many strong women of faith are mentioned in the Bible. The following are some of the more recognizable women of faith covered in this chapter:

- Sarah.
- Rebekah.
- Leah.
- Rahab.
- Deborah.
- Manoah's wife.
- Ruth.
- Hannah.
- Abigail.
- Esther.
- Elizabeth.
- Mary.
- Martha and Mary.

Who has not heard of Sarah? She was Abraham's wife, and her faith is recorded in Hebrews 11:11: "By faith Sarah herself also received strength to conceive seed, and she bore a child when she was past the age, because she judged Him faithful who had promised."

Who has not heard of Ruth? She was a Moabite woman who showed loyalty to her mother-in-law, Naomi, and her God. Her character and faith in God brought her many blessings, including being listed in the genealogy of Jesus Christ (Matthew 1:5). There are many other amazing women recorded in the Bible who were blessed by God because of their faith. It's important to remember and learn from these faithful women as well.

What is faith? Faith is "the substance of things hoped for, the evidence of things not seen" (Hebrews 11:1; see our article "What Is Faith?"). Sarah was well beyond the childbearing years, yet she bore Isaac just as God had said. She judged God to be faithful in what He had promised, and she was blessed because of her faith.

The Bible chronicles many such women of faith—women who believed and trusted in God. Their stories are found throughout the Scriptures.

For example, the story of Rahab is found in Joshua 2, and she—a gentile—is mentioned again in Hebrews 11:31 as having faith: "By faith the harlot Rahab did not perish with those who did not believe, when she had received the spies with peace." One of the most fascinating statements of faith is found in Hebrews 11:35:

"Women received their dead raised to life again."Examples abound of both Israelite and gentile women having faith. One of the most fascinating statements of faith is found in Hebrews 11:35: "Women received their dead raised to life again."

Who were those women? The author of Hebrews does not specifically say, but there are at least four women in the Bible who did witness the resurrection of their children. We may not often read their brief stories, but in each case, the faith of those women and those around them were increased, and reading of their experiences helps us also increase our faith in God. Some lesser-known women of faith in the Bible who received an amazing miracle

1. The widow of Zarephath. Her son had become very sick and died. Whereupon, Elijah the prophet "cried out to the LORD and said, 'O LORD my God, I pray, let this child's soul [life, New International Version] come back to him.' Then the LORD heard the voice of Elijah; and the soul of the child came back to him, and he revived. And Elijah took the child and brought him down from the upper room into the house, and gave him to his mother. And Elijah said, 'See, your son lives!' "Then the woman said to Elijah, 'Now by this I know that you are a man of God, and that the word of the LORD in your mouth is the truth'" (1 Kings 17:21-24).

2. The Shunammite woman. Her child was a miracle from God. She had been unable to conceive; but through God's blessing, she finally bore a son. When her son was young, he had a sudden illness and died. She laid him on the bed where Elisha slept when he traveled through the area. "When Elisha came into the house, there was the child, lying dead on his bed.

He went in therefore, shut the door behind the two of them, and prayed to the LORD. "And he went up and lay on the child, and put his mouth on his mouth, his eyes on his eyes, and his hands on his hands; and he stretched himself out on the child, and the flesh of the child became warm. He returned and walked back and forth in the house, and again went up and stretched himself out on him; then the child sneezed seven times, and the child opened his eyes.

"And he called Gehazi and said, 'Call this Shunammite woman.' So he called her. And when she came in to him, he said, 'Pick up your son.' So she went in, fell at his feet, and bowed to the ground; then she picked up her son and went out" (2 Kings 4:32-37).

3. The widow of Nain. This lady lost her only son. Jesus was moved with compassion and, for her sake, resurrected her son. "And when He came near the gate of the city, behold, a dead man was being carried out, the only son of his mother; and she was a widow. And a large crowd from the city was with her. When the Lord saw her, He had compassion on her and said to her, 'Do not weep.'

Then He came and touched the open coffin, and those who carried him stood still. And He said, 'Young man, I say to you, arise.' So he who was dead sat up and began to speak. And He presented him to his mother. "Then fear came upon all, and they glorified God, saying, 'A great prophet has risen up among us'; and, 'God has visited His people'" (Luke 7:12-16).

4. Jairus and his wife. Jairus was a ruler in a local synagogue. He and his wife were desperate since their only daughter was dying. So Jairus came to Jesus asking that their sick daughter be healed. On the way to their house, another faithful woman experienced a miracle by simply touching Jesus' clothing. "Now a certain woman had a flow of blood for twelve years, and had suffered many things from many physicians. She had spent all that she had and was no better, but rather grew worse.

"When she heard about Jesus, she came behind Him in the crowd and touched His garment. For she said, 'If only I may touch His clothes, I shall be made well.' Immediately the fountain of her blood was dried up, and she felt in her body that she was healed of the affliction.

And Jesus, immediately knowing in Himself that power had gone out of Him, turned around in the crowd and said, 'Who touched My clothes?' ... "But the woman, fearing and trembling, knowing what had happened to her, came and fell down before Him and told Him the whole truth. And He said to her, 'Daughter, your faith had made you well. Go in peace, and be healed of your affliction'" (Mark 5:25-30, 33-34). Just then some came from Jairus' house and said, "Your daughter is dead. Why trouble the Teacher any further?" (verse 35). But Jesus said, "Do not be afraid; only believe" (verse 36)

"He took the father and the mother of the child, and those who were with Him, and entered where the child was lying. Then He took the child by the hand, and said to her, 'Talitha, cumi,' which is translated, 'Little girl, I say to you, arise.' Immediately the girl arose and walked, for she was twelve years of age. And they were overcome with great amazement" (verses 40-42).

A woman's love for her children is very strong. These women "received their dead raised to life again" just as Hebrews 11:35 said. In these four cases, women observed their children's resurrections; and by what they and others saw, their faith was strengthened. How much greater will be the time when all women will receive their dead back to life? This is the promise Jesus gave His disciples, "Do not marvel at this; for the hour is coming in which all who are in the graves will hear His voice and come forth" (John 5:28-29).

That is the hope of all—the resurrection from the dead! It takes faith to believe this is going to happen! Characteristics of a woman of faith By studying these stories of faithful women mentioned in the Bible, we can learn what it takes to become such a woman. There are shared characteristics in their stories.

1. A woman of faith has a relationship with God. We must believe in and understand who God is. He is our Father, and He wants us to have a close relationship with Him. One way to accomplish that is by praying to Him regularly. The women of faith in the Bible did that often.

2. A woman of faith has a belief in God's words. God's words are life, and they give us encouragement and comfort. He wants us to consider what is in the Bible. It is important to read and meditate upon what God says. The women of faith in the Bible often knew what God had said and believed in His words.

3. A woman of faith has hope in the future. What does God plan for all of us? He wants us to be in His Kingdom. The stories of the four women who had their children raised from the dead can strengthen our faith and understanding of God's promise to resurrect the dead, and that God's Kingdom will come.

Other women of faith in the Bible .

The Bible records a number of other women who had faith, for example, Naomi, Jael, Mary Magdalene, Anna, Dorcas, Priscilla, Phoebe, Eunice and Lois. The story of these and other women of faith may be written in future articles. Please check this "Women of Faith" section often and learn how these women trusted in God and believed in His ways.

CHAPTER FOUR

STRANGE AND VIRTUOUS WOMEN

When woman was first created, she was made by God in a beautiful and sinless state. Due to her fall into sin, all women are now in one of two categories:The woman apart from God: The sinful woman who has not accepted Jesus Christ as Savior and received forgiveness for her sin. The woman of God: Once a sinner, this woman has confessed her sin and accepted Jesus Christ as Savior. She now stands virtuous (holy) before God.

The book of Proverbs in the Old Testament emphasizes the contrast between these two categories. The woman apart from God is referred to as the "strange" woman. The woman of God is referred to as the "virtuous" woman.The subject of the strange woman runs like a connecting thread throughout the book of Proverbs until the final chapter where the characteristics of the virtuous woman are presented as a glorious contrast.

THE BOOK OF PROVERBS

The book of Proverbs has been referred to as "vertical wisdom for horizontal living." It is a collection of wise principles given from God to man (vertically) to govern our living (horizontally) with others.The word "proverbs" means "a brief saying instead of many words." Each passage in Proverbs is a concise summary of an important truth.Solomon, the son of King David, wrote most of the Proverbs.

It is recorded in I Kings 4:32 that Solomon spoke three thousand proverbs under the inspiration of God. Some of these are preserved for us by the Holy Spirit in the book of Proverbs.Solomon's emphasis on strange and virtuous women developed in part from his own marriage relationships. Solomon sinned by marrying more than one wife and some of his wives were "strange" women who served false gods.

THE STRANGE WOMAN

The word "strange" in the book of Proverbs means "foreign, alien, adulterous." It describes a woman separated from God, a foreigner to His righteousness. Since God's ideal plan for woman is that she be part of His Body, the Church, this makes the strange woman an adulteress from God because she has turned from relationship with God to a sinful life.Proverbs identifies several characteristics of the "strange" woman. While all of these characteristics may not be evident, any of them can emerge in a sinful woman's life.

INSINCERE:The strange woman uses flattering speech, giving insincere praise with a wrong motive. Proverbs teaches that such a woman should be avoided:To deliver thee from the strange woman, even from the stranger which flattereth with her words. (Proverbs 2:16)To keep thee from ...the flattery of the tongue of a strange woman. (Proverbs 6:24)That they may keep thee from the strange woman, from the stranger which flattereth with her words. (Proverbs 7:5)

EVIL:One of the purposes of Proverbs is to provide principles....To keep thee from the evil woman. (Proverbs 6:24)

A DESTROYER:The strange woman seeks to destroy others by drawing them into her sin:For by means of a whorish woman a man is brought to a piece of bread; and the adulteress will hunt for the precious life. (Proverbs 6:26)

IMMODEST:The sinful woman dresses immodestly:And behold, there met him a woman with the attire of an harlot... (Proverbs 7:10)

SUBTLE:The strange woman is deceptive and subtitle:And behold, there met him a woman...subtitle of heart. (Proverbs 7:10)She is pictured as a deceptive pit which causes others to fall:For a whore is a deep ditch; and a strange woman is a narrow pit. (Proverbs 23:27)She speaks deceptive words which entice others to sin:For the lips of a strange woman drop as an honeycomb, and her mouth is smoother than oil. (Proverbs 5:3)

CONTENTIOUS:"Contentious" means to be argumentative, always involved in controversy:The contentions of a wife are a continual dropping. (Proverbs 19:13)A continual dropping on a very rainy day and a contentious woman are alike. (Proverbs 27:15) It is better to dwell in the wilderness than with a contentious and an angry woman. (Proverbs 21:19)

A BRAWLER: Two verses speak of the brawling of the strange woman. To "brawl" means to be loud and to fight noisily. Proverbs warns:It is better to dwell in the housetop than with a brawling woman in a wide house. (Proverbs 21:9)Even the corner of a housetop is more desirable:It is better to dwell in the corner of the housetop than with a brawling woman and in a wide house. (Proverbs 25:24)

ADULTEROUS:The sinful woman may be involved in adulterous physical relationships. For sure, she is an adulterous from God because she has neglected her relationship with Him:Such is the way of an adulterous woman... (Proverbs 30:20)And why wilt thou, my son, be ravished with a strange woman, and embrace the bosom of a stranger? (Proverbs 5:20)

SELF-RIGHTEOUS:The sinful woman does not comprehend her own true spiritual condition:...She eateth, and wipeth her mouth, and saith, I have done no wickedness. (Proverbs 30:20)

ODIOUS:Proverbs states that the strange woman is "odious" which means "hateful." The writer expresses concern...For an odious woman when she is married... (Proverbs 30:23)

ANGRY:It is better to dwell in the wilderness, than with a contentious and an angry woman. (Proverbs 21:19

UNPROFITABLE:Two verses reveal a strange woman can cause financial ruin:Take his garment that is surety for a stranger, and take a pledge of him for a strange woman. (Proverbs 27:13 and 20:16)

FOOLISH AND CLAMOROUS:To be foolish is to lack wisdom. "Clamorous" means to loudly complain and demand:A foolish woman is clamorous... (Proverbs 9:13)

UNKNOWLEDGEABLE:A foolish woman is clamorous; she is simple, and knoweth nothing. (Proverbs 9:13)

WITHOUT DISCRETION:This means she has no tact. Proverbs compares a beautiful woman without discretion to a jewel in the nose of a pig: As a jewel of gold in a swine's snout, so is a fair woman which is without discretion. (Proverbs 11:22)The book of Proverbs describes the strange woman as a rather unpleasant person. It is better to dwell in the housetop (Proverbs 21:9), in the wilderness (Proverbs 21:19), or in the corner of the housetop (Proverbs 25:24) than to dwell with her.

Strange (foolish)

- Destroys her home (14:1)
- Clamorous, simple, knows nothing (9:13)
- Like a jewel in a swine's snout (11:22)

Virtuous(Wise)

- Builds her home. (14:1)
- Retains honor (11:16)
- Crown to her husband (12:4)

WOMAN AS WIFE

Proverbs makes several observations regarding the woman's role as a wife. These comments continue to develop the contrast between strange and virtuous women:A virtuous woman is a crown to her husband; but she that maketh ashamed is as rottenness to his bones. (Proverbs 12:4)

Men are warned against adulterous relationships with women:So he that goeth in to his neighbors' wife; whosoever toucheth her shall not be innocent. (Proverbs 6:29)But whoso committeth adultery with a woman lacketh understanding; he that doeth it destroyeth his own soul. (Proverbs 6:32)

A man is to be satisfied with his own wife rather than strange women:Let thy fountain be blessed and rejoice with the wife of thy youth. (Proverbs 5:18)A virtuous wife is a gift from the Lord:Whoso findeth a wife findeth a good thing, and obtaineth favour of the Lord. (Proverbs 18:22)...a prudent wife is from the Lord. (Proverbs 19:14) A strange wife is contentious and a continuing trial:...the contentions of a wife are a continual dropping. (Proverbs 19:13)

THE VIRTUOUS WOMAN

After describing the strange woman throughout the Proverbs, the writer closes with a glorious contrast of the virtuous woman. The discussion opens with a question and a declaration: Who can find a virtuous woman? for her price is far above rubies. (Proverbs 31:10)

Read Proverbs 31:10-31 which details the characteristics of the virtuous woman. Keep your Bible open to this passage as you review her personality traits. Remember, just as the sinful woman may not exhibit all of the traits of the strange woman, the following characteristics may not all be apparent in a Godly woman. They can be attained through spiritual growth, however, and are God's picture of the ideal woman.The following is a verse-by-verse study of the characteristics of the virtuous woman

VERSE 10:The virtuous woman is rare, as the writer questions "Who can find a virtuous woman?" To be virtuous means to be morally good. This kind of woman is awarded eternal value, far above rubies. The Amplified Bible expands this verse to include the characteristics of intelligence and capability.

VERSE 11:She is trustworthy and the heart of her husband safely trusts in her.

VERSE 12:Her relationships are right. She wants only good for her husband. The Amplified Bible expands the meaning of "good" to include the concepts of comforting and encouraging her husband. VERSE 13:She is industrious and a willing worker.

VERSE 14: She provides for her household. This verse means spiritual as well as physical provision. The Amplified

Bible expands this passage to explain that she provides for the "physical, material, and spiritual needs of her household."

VERSE 15:She is considerate and responsible. She rises early to make provision for her family. This is also a type of making spiritual provision by rising early to meet with God. The virtuous woman is a good supervisor and she provides for those who work for her.

VERSE 16:She is businesslike. She considers, plans, and thinks before she acts. She is aggressive and productive in the "vineyard" or work God has given her to do. The Amplified Bible indicates she doesn't neglect her present duties by assuming others. She expands prudently (wisely).

VERSE 17:The virtuous woman is strong. The Amplified Version states she develops "spiritual, mental, and physical fitness for her God given task."

VERSE 18:She has a good self image and is not affected by outward circumstances. According to the Amplified Bible, her light of encouragement burns in the night of trouble and sorrow, warding off fear, doubt, and distrust.

VERSE 19:She is skillful and trained for her work. She knows how to use the "tools of her trade," so to speak.

VERSE 20:The virtuous woman is generous to the poor and reaches out to minister to the needy. The Amplified Bible says she "ministers to the body, mind, and spirit of others."

VERSE 21:The virtuous woman is fearless. She clothes her family, not only physically but spiritually. Hebrews 9:19-21 speaks of the spiritual covering of the blood of Jesus Christ.

VERSE 22:This passage describes the virtuous woman as a creative homemaker as well as being properly dressed.

VERSE 23:She is supportive of her husband's position.

VERSE 24:She is a good business woman.

VERSE 25:She is strong, honorable, and joyfully looks to the future.

VERSE 26:She is wise and ministers through the spoken word. She controls her tongue and is kind.

VERSE 27:She is conscientious (responsible) and looks well to the ways of her household. She is not idle, but is active and energetic. The Amplified Bible states she "does not eat the bread of idle gossip, discontent, and self-pity. "

VERSE 28:The virtuous woman is an ideal wife and mother.

VERSE 29:She "excels in virtue." The spirit of excellence is apparent in her life and ministry.

VERSE 30:She is successful and others recognize it. She also fears God.

VERSE 31:She will be fruitful (productive) and others will honor her for her contributions. Her own works praise her. She does not have to boast.

THE SECRET OF THE VIRTUOUS WOMAN

What is the secret of the virtuous woman? How can she achieve all of these positive traits? She fears the Lord! All of her righteousness, all of her wonderful positive character traits spring from her right relationship with God. Fearing God involves more than respecting Him. It includes acknowledging Him as God, recognizing and confessing your sin, and accepting Jesus Christ as personal Savior.

As you become a new creature in Jesus Christ, all the old things are done away with:Therefore if any man be in Christ, he is a new creature: old things are passed away; behold, all things are become new. (II Corinthians 5:17) The virtuous woman was once affected by the sin which came upon all men and women through Eve's original sin.

The difference between her and the sinful woman is that she is no longer sinful. She has been cleansed by the saving power of Christ. Your life may be ruined by sin. You may have many of the characteristics of the sinful woman evident in your life.

Right now, through Christ, you can be transformed from a sinful to a virtuous woman. You can restore your relationship with God and then let Him develop these beautiful, virtuous characteristics in your life. All you have to do is confess your sins and accept Jesus Christ as your Savior. If you have not already made this commitment, pray to God in your own words and do this right now

CHAPTER FIVE

THE BOOK OF RUTH

INTRODUCTION

There are two books in the Bible that are named for women. They are the books of Ruth and Esther. In this chapter we will study the book of Ruth, the Gentile woman who served God among the Jewish people. In the next chapter, we will study about Esther, the Jewish woman who served God among the Gentiles. Before proceeding further with this chapter, read the four chapters of the book of Ruth.

This book is named for Ruth, the Moabite daughter-in-law of Naomi, who was a Jew. Moabites were descendants of Lot and were heathen people. Ruth is one of four women mentioned in Matthew 1 as ancestors of Jesus who were part of the Messianic family line. The other three women are Tamar, Rahab, and Bathsheba

AUTHOR : The author of this book is not known.

TIME: The time of the events of the book of Ruth is identified in the first verse of the first chapter. The story occurred during the period of the judges of Israel which was a time of trouble in the history of God's people, Israel.

There was no king in Israel and the people turned away from God to live as they pleased:In those days there was no king in Israel, but every man did that which was right in his own eyes. (Judges 17:6)The book of Judges records this dark period in Israel's history. The people sinned repeatedly, experienced God's judgment, and turned back to God for deliverance. Each time God raised up a judge (a Godly leader) to deliver them. .

CHARACTERS The main characters in the book of Ruth are: Naomi: An Israelite woman who migrated to Moab with her husband and two sons to escape a famine in Israel.

Elimelech: Husband of Naomi who died in Moab.

Mahlon and Chilion: Sons of Naomi who died in Moab .

Orpha: The Moabite daughter-in-law of Naomi who chose to remain in Moab.

Ruth: The Moabite daughter-in-law of Naomi who returned to Israel with her.

Boaz: The son of the harlot Rahab. He was the near kinsman who redeemed Ruth and became her husband.

The unnamed kinsman: A nameless man who legally had the first right to redeem the property of Naomi and make Ruth his wife, but who chose not to do so.

Purpose

While it is true that a purpose of the book of Ruth could be the example of those who were faithful to Goddespite living in cruel and idolatrous times, it is likely that the main purpose of this book is revealed to us inits last chapter. We are given divine information of the origin and lineage of the family of David (4:17-22).As already noted, this is especially important given its Messianic implications.

Outline

A) The Sojourn In Moab (1:1-13)

B) Ruth's Loyalty And Commitment (1:14-22)

C) Gleaning In The Field Of Boaz (2:1-23)

D) Boaz Accepts The Role Of A Kinsman (3:1-18)

E) Boaz Redeems Ruth (4:1-12)

F) The Marriage Of Boaz And Ruth (4:13-22).

Powerfull lessons we can learn from book of Ruth

• Loss Is Hard : The book of Ruth starts with the life of Naomi. Naomi was from Bethlehem and moved to Moab with her husband Elimelek and two sons, Mahlon and Kilion. Naomi, later on, lost her husband and she was left with her two sons. Her two sons found wives, Ruth and Orpah, but 10 years later, both sons died as well. Talk about a hard time, right? It was then that Naomi decided to return back home to the land of Judah. Because Naomi had lost her husband and sons, she was moving back home to Bethlehem as a widow. Her heart and life had crumbled. This is a reminder that loss and change are hard and, unfortunately, it's more common than we know. Many times while dealing with grief we can feel lost or forgotten. Naomi knew all too well how that felt.

• Keep Your Commitments

Ruth and Orpah were both given the blessing from Naomi to go back to their hometowns after their husbands had passed. Naomi knew she couldn't provide the women with new husbands and she wanted them to take the obvious choice for "moving forward" for another marriage if it was God's will. Orpah took the option but Ruth decided to stay with Naomi and head to Bethlehem together. "Where you go I will go, and where you stay I will stay. Your people will be my people and your God my God." (Ruth 1:16) How many times have we made choices to be in a place that we "think" will give us what we want? Ruth was brave in keeping her commitment to Naomi, staying with her instead of looking to her own interests

• Bitterness Happens

When Naomi and Ruth made it to Bethlehem, townswomen stated, "Can this be Naomi?" (Ruth 1:19) But when Naomi, which name means "pleasant," heard she answered with, "Don't call me Naomi," she told them. "Call me Mara, because the Almighty has made my life very bitter. I went away full, but the Lord has brought me back empty. Why call me Naomi? The Lord has afflicted me; the Almighty has brought misfortune upon me." (Ruth 1:20-21).

Needless to say, Naomi was upset. She knew that she had been blessed to have her husband and sons, and then she felt like God just took everything away from her. Returning to her hometown, she felt less-than, empty, and bitter for what had happened to her. Have you ever felt that way? Bitter and mad at God for what may feel like a ruined life? You're not alone

• Get to Work

When they had reached their new home, Ruth decided to get to work. "And Ruth the Moabite said to Naomi, "Let me go to the fields and pick up the leftover grain behind anyone in whose eyes I find favor." (Ruth 2:2) She was in a new town, with new people, and wanted to help take care of Naomi and herself.

She decided to glean in a nearby field and follow the harvesters. Her work ethic did not go unnoticed as a foreman would speak about her labor to Boaz shortly after his notice of her: "She's been at it steady ever since, from early morning until now, without so much as a break." (Ruth 2:7 MSG)

• Honorable Intentions

After her introduction, Boaz tells Ruth to not "... glean in another field and don't go away from here. Stay here with the women who work for me." (Ruth 2:8). Later on in the chapter, we understand more fully how much Boaz's first reaction of Ruth was to protect her as Naomi explains, "It will be good for you, my daughter, to go with the women who work for him, because in someone else's field you might be harmed." (Ruth 2:22). Boaz's first reaction to Ruth was not in charm but in protection.

• She Made a Move

Naomi wanted Ruth to find a home where she can be provided for. Naomi believed Boaz to be the guardian-redeemer in her family line. She told Ruth to get dressed up in her best clothes and perfume and go to Boaz. Ruth did just that. She let Boaz know of her interest by lying at his feet after he had fallen asleep. When he woke up and asked what she was doing she stated, "I am your servant Ruth," she said. "Spread the corner of your garment over me, since you are a guardian-redeemer of our family." (Ruth 3:9) Talk about letting a man know you are interested, right?!

• Noble Character is Important

As Ruth went to Boaz to ask for his covering, he knew there was another man in line ahead of him for Naomi's land. He stated that if the man wanted to be her guardian-redeemer, then he would have the rights to her land and her hand, but if not, then Boaz was more than happy to oblige.

He didn't let Ruth just leave after their conversation in the middle of the night to protect her reputation because she was a "woman of noble character." He was a gentleman even in a vulnerable position and did the right thing. She rested at his feet until dawn and left when no one would notice her. On top of that, he didn't let her leave empty-handed as he gave her and Naomi 6 measures of barley!

• Our Decisions Matter

After Boaz purchased the land and acquired Ruth's hand in marriage, they became pregnant with a son. This son was named Obed who later became the father of Jesse who later became the father of David who, as we know, is in the direct family line of Jesus Christ! How awesome to see how the braveness and commitment of a young woman would later meet a man that would help to bring the family lines of Jesus Christ into fruition.

God also brought joy back to Naomi as she lovingly helped to take care of Obed! How awesome is our God that He can take such a dark and lonely season for Naomi and Ruth and turn it into joy, love, and prosperity! Never underestimate the power of your decisions, commitment, humility, and integrity!

CHAPTER SIX

THE BOOK OF ESTHER

INTRODUCTION

In the last chapter you studied the Book of Ruth, the Gentile woman who lived among the Jewish people. This chapter focuses on Esther, the Jewish woman who served as queen among the Gentile people. The book which bears her name tells of a plot to destroy the entire Jewish nation which would have ended the blood line of the Messiah, Jesus Christ.Although the book does not mention God by name, it speaks of His intervention in the affairs of men to care for His people and accomplish His divine purposes.

It also shows how each one of us has an important part in God's plan. Before proceeding with this study, read the book of Esther. The book is named for the main character, Esther. Originally her Hebrew name was Hadassah. Her name means "star of the east."

AUTHOR The author of the book is unknown.

TIME From the best evidence, the story of Esther occurred during the rule of the king who is known in secular history as Xerxes. In Esther, the name used for this king is Ahasuerus, the Hebrew form of the Greek name

Xerxes. The nature of the court, social customs, and state of affairs described in Esther fit perfectly into the secular history of this time which was around 473 B.C.

MAIN CHARACTERS Ahasuerus: King over 127 provinces from India to Ethiopia.

Vashti: The queen who refused the king's orders and lost her position as queen.

Esther: The new queen, a Hebrew woman.

Mordecai: Esther's cousin, who raised her from a child.

Haman: An enemy of the Jewish people who devised a plot to destroy them.

PURPOSES

The purposes of Esther:1. The book contains an important episode in Jewish history which provided the Jewish people of Persia and Palestine with the story of the intervention of God to spare their live

2. It demonstrates how God works for His people. He intervenes in the affairs of men to fulfill His will and places His people in the right places at the right times for the advancement of His Kingdom.

OUTLINE

• I. The wife who refused to obey her husband, Chapter 1

• II. The beauty contest to choose a real queen, Chapter 2

• Haman and anti-Semitism, Chapter 3

• For such a time as this, Chapter 4

• The scepter of grace and the nobility of Esther, Chapter 5

• When a king could not sleep at night, Chapter 6

• The man who came to dinner but died on the gallows, Chapter 7

• The message of hope that went out from the king, Chapter 8

• The institution of the Feast of Purim, Chapters 9, 10

Powerfull lessons we can learn from book of EstherGod is the only One who has the power to turn trials into blessings. Don't ever doubt that He is able. Nothing is impossible with Him. This story has his miraculous work and power all over it, through every chapter, every word.

There is a constant thread of redemption through Esther's story that speaks to our lives still today. Things in life hadn't gone Esther's way. Often, we may read this story and just think of Esther being beautiful and given the royal position of Queen. Yet we forget where she came from.

She was orphaned. She had suffered great loss, even at a young age. She was then whisked away from her home, her family, her people, and all she knew; and she was taken to the King's palace, given the load of expectation to succeed. Yet even when gifted with such a royal position, there was still incredible hardship. Her people faced great tragedy and destruction. She surely felt very alone.

She faced trial after trial through her life, yet we see in every part of the story, there is hope woven through. And it's truly the most powerful piece of the entire book. God is always at work even when we can't see the whole story. Even when things look uncertain. And that sets the stage for great things to happen, "...And who knows but that you have come to royal position for such a time as this?" Esther 4:14. God's blessings are greater than our troubles. Always. His goodness will shine through. It's just the way He works

• Our prayers matter. Our voice matters. Our actions matter. And God is our Deliverer. We can choose to live with grace and kindness. We can choose to stay involved, to have a voice, to be engaged, and to make a difference in our nation and the world. Mordecai knew his voice mattered. Esther knew her actions mattered. And through the wisdom and obedience of these two, God saved his people.

Mordecai believed that even if Esther didn't help them, God would send help from a different way, that's how much he trusted in the power of the Lord. He understood that our positions in life were not at all about us, but only about what God could do through those powerful places. "For if you remain silent at this time, relief and deliverance for the Jews will arise from another place, but you and your father's family will perish..." Esther 4:14.

May God help us to be willing to pray, fast, wait for His direction, then act on the wisdom He provides. May we be ever faithful to pray for all those in authority, for those who need someone to speak up on their behalf, for those who are being pressed down or persecuted. May we be brave to speak with wisdom and discernment, and to live these days with hearts of compassion and love. May we be strong to follow God's voice, even when it's not the most popular choice in our culture. Because sometimes He works through that and surprises everyone

• God will give us the courage to do all that He asks us to do. Obedience to His call is vital. It may even have the power to affect an entire generation of people. We may never be fully aware of how our actions and faithfulness to His voice are working so powerfully in those around us. We don't have to stay stuck in fear. We don't need to run from his leading, even when we feel incredibly unprepared or inadequate for the job.

He will equip us for every task and will pave the way for us to walk through with His power, providing grace for every step and covering us from behind. Queen Esther had a choice. When Mordecai sent word to her about the great danger their people were facing, she could have simply tried to save herself. She could have kept quiet, just hoped for the best, or turned the other way. But she and Mordecai both knew that God had given her great purpose in her position.

She was wise; she made a plan and didn't stay stuck in fear or worry. She prayed and fasted, and she asked for their people to do the same. She was willing to act, to follow God's lead, and to save the lives of her people, even if it meant she might lose hers. "Then Esther sent this reply to Mordecai: 'Go, gather together all the Jews who are in Susa, and fast for me. Do not eat or drink for three days, night or day. I and my maids will fast as you do. When this is done, I will go to the king, even though it is against the law. And if I perish, I perish,'" Esther 4:15-16. Though our current situations may look different than what Esther faced, we might still be struggling with great fear or uncertainty. The future may look dark.

A hard diagnosis or recent loss may have sent us spiraling. Yet often God places us in positions of influence, or in strategic locations, with great purpose in mind. Many times, the places where we find ourselves are not really all about us. It's about Him. It's about His bigger plan.

• God will always be faithful to lead us and to fight on our behalf. He is forever faithful, and this story is a great testimony of that. Sometimes He tells us to wait. Other times He will say to move quickly. We must be so in tune with His leadership and His Spirit within us, that we can recognize what He's saying. His timing is perfect, always.

Even when it's not our timing. Even when things seem "off," or we start to feel forgotten. God is at work, often in ways we can't fully see. His timing is laying out every crucial plan at just the right minute. It's never haphazard or thrown together. It's intricately woven into the stories and purposes of our entire lives. As Queen Esther and Mordecai moved through these critical days and worked on behalf of their people, every plan was carefully timed, and each purpose was carried out to the glory of the Lord. In the end, the tables were turned. Those who were plotting against the Jews were destroyed. "No one could stand against them, because the people of all other nationalities were afraid of them," Esther 9:2.

The plan to kill the Jews had been stopped. There was great fear of God all around, His reputation became known throughout the land, even to the point that "many people of other nationalities even became Jews because fear of the Jews had seized them," Esther 8:17. With God, even our enemies will flee. His power can never be thwarted or destroyed.

He is with us, guiding us, carrying us, and covering us from behind at every moment. May God help us to follow His lead, believing that His timing is perfect and remembering that He's always faithful to fight for us, still today. May He help us to know when to keep quiet and wait, and when to speak out on behalf of others, and in sharing His truth. He won't leave us on our own to fend for ourselves in difficult places. His power can't help but to come to our rescue. His faithfulness and mercies are new every morning.

• Pride is a trap. Humility is key. This is a huge lesson in the story of Esther: pride is a trap and will lead to our demise. Every character through this book had to decide whether they would choose to live with pride or humility. Those who chose pride faced final defeat. Those who walked with humility and integrity before God rose above every hard circumstance with His grace and power.

By the time Mordecai told Esther about the evil plot against the Jews, Esther was in high places. She could have turned her back on her people, proud of where she was in life and happy about her own success and power. Yet she did just the opposite. That is true humility. Being willing to look at the needs of others before yourself, not thinking too highly of yourself, even if the world would say you have much to be proud of. Haman chose just the opposite.

He devised a plan to ultimately make himself look better and destroy a people who wouldn't bend a knee to him. He was proud and full of selfishness and hate. Ultimately, it destroyed him. The whole story plays out like a great movie plot. It's amazing how God used every bit of Haman's evil plan to turn it back on his own life. The Jews were saved, and Mordecai was given honor

CHAPTER SEVEN

DEBORAH

Who Was Deborah in the Bible?

Deborah is one of the most influential women of the Bible. As a prophet, Judge Deborah was said to hear God's voice and share God's Word with others. As a priestess, she did not offer sacrifices, as the men did, but she did lead worship services and preach.

Deborah is one of the most influential women of the Bible. She is known for her wisdom and courage and is the only woman of the Old Testament who is known for her own faith and action, not because of her relationship to her husband or another man.

As a prophet, Judge Deborah was said to hear God's voice and share God's Word with others. As a priestess, she did not offer sacrifices, as the men did, but she did lead worship services and preach.

Many biblical scholars believe that Deborah was a wife, as well. However, in Hebrew, the same word is used for "woman" and "wife," so we don't know, with certainty, if Deborah was a "woman of Lappidoth" (a place) or the "wife of Lappidoth" (a person).

Facts about Deborah in the Bible

Her story is told in both prose (Judges 4) and poetry (Judges 5).Deborah has an impressive resume of judge, warrior, poet, and prophet as well as singer and songwriter.

She was only one of five women described as a prophet in the Old Testament. The four others are Miriam, Huldah (2 Kings 22:14, 2 Chronicles 34:22), Noadiah (Nehemiah 6:14), and "the prophetess" (Isaiah 8:3).The only other person in the Bible who was said to be both prophet and judge was Samuel.Deborah is the only female judge mentioned in the Bible.

Meaning of Deborah's Name

Deborah, (Devorah or D'vorah in Hebrew) is translated as "bee."The Midrash (a collection of teachings on the Torah) explains that the Hebrew people are said to be like bees in several ways:

1. Just as bees follow their leader in a swarm, the Jewish people follow the sages and prophets to teach them.

2. As a bee sting is quite painful, but the bee's honey is incredibly sweet, God's Word will sting those who don't follow His commands but will bless those who live righteously with a sweet life.

3. Bees collect pollen and nectar, not for their own benefit, but for the benefit of others, just as the Hebrews collect mitzvahs (a good deed done for others or religious benefit) for the Lord's pleasure and benefit.

4. Bees are a lowly insect, which is a reminder to God's children to be humble.

Deborah's Roles as Judge and Warrior

Deborah the Judge

Judge Deborah was one of the rulers of the Hebrews (and the only female leader) in the Old Testament. These rulers were called "mishpat," which is translated as "judges." A role that originated back when Moses appointed helpers to assist him in resolving arguments among the people. (Exodus 18).

Judges sought guidance from the Lord by praying and meditating before proclaiming their ruling on a matter. Many of the judges were also thought of as prophets who articulated "a word from the Lord."Deborah would sit under the palm tree between Ramah and Bethel in the hill country of Ephraim; and the Israelites would line up for her to rule on a matter.

Deborah the Warrior

Deborah, upon receiving instructions from God, called Barak, an Israelite warrior, to bring 10,000 troops up Mount Tabor to attack Sisera, Jabin's commander of troops.

Barak responded by saying "If you will go with me, I will go; if not I will not go" (Judges 4:8).

In the next verse, Deborah agrees to go to battle with Barak and the troops but share with him: "However, there will be no glory for you in the course you are taking, for then the Lord will deliver Sisera into the hands of a woman" (Judges 4:9).

Judge and warrior Deborah went off to battle with Barak, and, as foretold in prophecy, Sisera fell at the hands of a woman – but not Deborah. Rather it was Jael, the wife of a clan leader, who would avenge the Israelites by driving a tent peg through Sisera's head with a mallet when he asked for water and respite.

Biblical commentaries and scholars disagree on Barak's acceptance of Deborah's battle leadership. Some feel that Barak respected her as a leader and prophetess and willingly heeded her call. Others, however, concluded that his response in Judges 4:8 pointed to his discomfort in taking orders from a woman, despite the esteem she is held in.

What can we learn from Deborah's story?

Deborah, and her story, can teach us so much, but there are three lessons we can all learn from:

1. Be Obedient

If God is telling you to do something or go somewhere, despite your fears, listen to His call. He has plans that we cannot begin to understand, and hearts and lives may be changed by our obedience.

2. Be Courageous

The old saying "God doesn't call the qualified, He qualifies the called" applies here. Doing something out of your comfort zone to glorify Him can be terrifying, but faith was never promised to be easy. Be bold. Be courageous - for His glory.

3. Stand True

Never waiver in your faith. We may not always know what the road ahead will look like, but we only need to remember that God will faithfully guide us and lead the way.

CHAPTER EIGHT

WOMEN IN THE BOOK OF ACTS

These all with one mind were continually devoting themselves to prayer, along with the women, and Mary the mother of Jesus, and with His brothers. (Acts 1:14) From its opening chapters, the book of Acts seemingly presents women equivalently in status with the men at the formation of the church.

1 After seeing Christ taken up, the apostles and other followers find themselves gathered with women, including Christ's mother, in a house in Jerusalem – Acts 1:12-14. All those gathered prayed together leading up to the famous moment of Pentecost. The language which is laying the foundation of the book shows women to be active participants in the prayer gathering with even the great male apostles.

As the author of Acts moves into the second chapter and the Holy Spirit comes upon the people, there is no reason offered to suppose the same women seen in the upper room previously are not included in the "all of them were filled with the Holy Spirit..." – Acts 2:4.

Thus, women are seen participating in one of the greatest kick off events of the church, not only as equal in prayer, but equal in receipt of God's Spirit. That the women were filled with the Holy Spirit and were also speaking in tongues on public display, is further supported in Peter's subsequent sermon.

He tells the crowd that they are seeing the fulfillment of the last days where God's Spirit will come upon "sons and... ...daughters..., both men and women..." – Acts 2:18. Certainly for God's word to be declared 100% true by Peter and recognized by his audience, it would necessarily have been completely fulfilled at that time with both sexes being represented as the prophecy required.

Moving on from equal inclusion in the launch of the church, women are seen as equal in conversion. The book of Acts does not speak of subservient woman who followed their converted husbands into the man's choice of belief. Rather, the book speaks with terms of equality of simply both men and women becoming believers – Acts 5:14.

The principle of self-agency in the salvation of women is shown further with the distinction that both men and women are spoken of individually as being baptized – Acts 8:12. Furthermore, women are equally demonstrated as recipients of miracles and workers of good works. A woman, Tabitha, is even raised from the dead. This woman is spoken of with the term disciple, and is told to have been very charitable – Acts 9:36, 40.

Another woman, Mary, is seen as instrumental in providing her house as a meeting place for the church – Acts 12:12. Perhaps the most blatant work a woman is shown to have done for the church is to correct Apollos, an experienced public speaker, in his understanding of Christian doctrine. Pricilla and Aquila, wife and husband, are both seen to be involved in the correction of Apollos, but the order of names as written in Acts names Pricilla first, seemingly giving her the prominent position in the act of correction – Acts 18:24, 26.

Alongside the positive light Acts places upon women next to the men, the book also presents women as equal in persecution received and given. Saul is seen to have given no preferential treatment to women over men when he persecuted the church, but punishing them both – Acts 22:4. On the other hand, women of high status are shown just as involved as the "chief men" in persecution of the apostles – Acts 13:50.

MEMBERS OF THE CHURCH

In most places where the Gospel was preached, women (both Jew and Gentile) are mentioned as being among those who believed. In Jerusalem, multitudes of both men and women believed. (Acts 5:14). In Samaria, both men and women believed as a result of Philip's preaching (Acts 8:12). At Joppa, Dorcas and other women were members of the early Church (Acts 9:36-43).

At Lystra lived Timothy's mother Eunice and grandmother who were believers (Acts 16:1).At Philippi, Lydia became the first Christian convert in Europe and there were other unnamed women who were part of the Church there (Acts 16:13-15).

In Thessalonica and Berea many of the chief women believed (Acts 17:4,12). The greatest number of women believers mentioned were in Macedonia. Even in Athens where response to Paul's preaching was minimal, a woman named Damaris and others believed (Acts 17:34).These women were not just passive audiences. They were true believers in the Gospel and were baptized into the Church:But when they believed Philip preaching the things concerning the kingdom of God, and the name of Jesus Christ, they were baptized, both men and women. (Acts 8:12)

INTERCESSORS

Women in the early Church were intercessors in prayer. Mary, the mother of Jesus, joined the men in prayer waiting for the coming of the Holy Spirit:These all continued with one accord in prayer and supplication, with the women and Mary, the mother of Jesus, and with his brethren. (Acts 1:14)

When Peter was put in prison by Herod, the believers were praying in the home of Mary, the mother of John Mark. Rhoda, one of the women in the prayer meeting, met Peter at the door after the angel delivered him from the jail and carried news of the victory to others at the prayer meeting (Acts 12:12-16).

In the city of Philippi, a group of women met by the river to pray: And on the sabbath we went out of the city by a river side, where prayer was wont to be made, and we sat down, and spake unto the women which resorted there. (Acts 16:13)The phrase "wont to be made" means that it was the habit of the women to gather there for prayer.

SUPPORTERS OF GOD'S WORK

Women in Acts provided material support to the work of God. Lydia provided lodging to Paul's missionary team. Dorcas had a ministry to widow women which included providing them with clothing. In Corinth, Paul lived in the home of Priscilla, who not only shared in her husband Aquila's business but also had an important place in the Corinthian Church. They allowed Paul to share in their business during his stay in Corinth.

RESPONSIBLE SINNERS

Women were held accountable for sin. Perhaps the most tragic story involving a woman is the account in Acts 5:1-11 of a woman named Sapphira who joined her husband in a deceitful plan concerning money. As you read this story, note that it is an opposite situation to that of Adam and Eve. Here, Satan put the scheme in the husband's heart and Sapphira joined him in the plan. Sapphira was held equally guilty because she had full knowledge of her husband's sin and joined him in it.

In moral issues, a woman cannot be blindly obedient to a husband and use the claim of submission to him to excuse her sin.The same standard of holiness is expected from every follower of Christ, whether male or female

CHAPTER NINE

WOMEN IN THE BOOK OF EPISTLES

Therefore they that were scattered abroad went every where preaching the Word. (Acts 8:4) "Women In The Epistles." In This chapter discusses women with specific ministries who are mentioned in these books. We will discusses the general position of women in the early Church as taught by the Epistles.And finally we will discuss in this chapter on "Women In The Epistles" focuses on special categories of women addressed by these books, (i.e., single, widowed, married, young, old, mothers, etc.) and special instructions regarding the dress and disposition of women.

THE EPISTLES The New Testament consists of four major divisions. These include the Gospels, which are the books of Matthew, Mark, Luke and John which tell of the life and ministry of Jesus Christ.Acts is a special division which describes the formation of the early Church. There is one book of prophecy which is the final book in the New Testament. It is called Revelation.

All the other New Testament books are called Epistles because they were written to specific believers in a letter type format. They are an inspired part of the Word of God and applicable to all believers in addition to those to whom they were specifically addressed.

The following is a list of the Epistles and the names of the authors credited with writing them under the inspiration of the Holy Spirit:These Epistles were all written by the Apostle Paul, Romans, I Corinthians ,II Corinthians ,Galatians Ephesians ,Philippians, Colossians, I Thessalonians ,II Thessalonians ,I Timothy II Timothy, Titus, Philemon ,Hebrews

These books were named for the person who wrote them James, I Peter ,II Peter, I John, II John, III John, Jude.

WOMEN WITH MINISTRIES IN THE EPISTLESWOMEN IN ROME:

Phoebe carried the great doctrinal statement of the book of Romans to the believers in Rome. In the original Greek text, Phoebe is referred to as a "diakonos." This word appears 22 times in the New Testament. In 18 of these, translators render it "minister" and three times as "deacon." In Phoebe's case, they change it to servant, perhaps reflecting bias on the part of the translators.

In introducing Phoebe to the believers in Rome, Paul says to:...receive her in the Lord, as becometh saints, and that ye assist her in whatsoever business she hath need of you: for she has been a succourer of many, and of myself also. (Romans 16:2)

Some have thought from this passage that Phoebe provided hospitality to Paul, fed him, did his laundry, etc. But the word "succourer" actually means helper and the feminine form of the word means "one who stands before, a chief leader." The consideration Paul requests is the same he asks for male leaders and elders in I Thessalonians 5:12-13 and I Timothy 5:17.In Romans 16, Paul refers to another woman in Rome, Prisca, who is married to Aquila.

This is the same woman called Priscilla by Luke. Prisca is the more formal form of her name. We already studied about this woman in Chapter Eight.The word "helper" which Paul used to describe her means "fellow worker." Paul stressed that Prisca and Aquila not only risked their lives but were also involved in an important ministry to the Gentile Churches. Other women on Paul's list at Rome include Mary, who worked hard for the believers; Narcissus, who seemed to be the head of a household; Tryphena and Tryphosa, whose names mean dainty and delicate; and "the beloved Persis" who also worked hard in the Lord.

There is a woman named Julia, about whom we are told nothing, and two other women whose names are not given, the mother of Rufus and the sister of Nereus. Junia, mentioned in Romans 16:7, was noted by the apostles for her faith, and was a fellow prisoner with Paul for the cause of Christ.

WOMEN IN THE OTHER EPISTLES:

Chloe is mentioned in I Corinthians 1:11. She sent a report to Paul about some disturbing things going on in the Church at Corinth. In Philemon, Paul addresses Apphia, Philemon's wife. This couple had a Church in their home as did Lydia and Nympha. Euodia and Syntyche mentioned in Philippians 4:2 may have done evangelistic work, since Paul describes them as "those women which labored (struggled) with me in the Gospel...with my other fellow laborers."

Paul extends greetings from "Claudia and all the brethren" in II Timothy 4:21 although we are not told anything about this woman.

TEACHING AND PREACHING

One of the difficult passages in the Epistles affecting the role of women in the Church is in I Corinthians:For God is not the author of confusion, but of peace, as in all Churches of the saints.Let your women keep silence in the Churches; for it is not permitted unto them to speak; but they are commanded to be under obedience, as also saith the law.

And if they will learn any thing, let them ask their husbands at home: for it is a shame for women to speak in the Church. (I Corinthians 14:33-35) This passage is often used to prohibit women from teaching or preaching in the Church. Paul does not mean women are to keep totally silent. In the preceding chapter, he provides much detail about how a woman should have her head covered when she prays and prophesies. (We will discuss this passage later in this chapter).

Why would he waste time on this discussion if they were not supposed to speak in Church at all?In the study on Acts you learned that at the coming of the Holy Spirit Peter said it fulfilled the prophecy of Joel. This prophecy stated the Holy Spirit was to come upon the "daughters and handmaidens" and they would prophesy.I Corinthians 14 may be one of the passages that Peter refers to as "difficult to understand" in Paul's writings.

The most important clue to the problem is the meaning of the Greek word translated "to speak" in verse 34. The word here does not refer to public speaking, but means "chatting, questioning, arguing." Read I Corinthians 14 in your Bible. You will note that Paul's purpose in this chapter is to prevent confusion in the Church. His concern is that everything is done in order in the worship services.

This is why he tells women not to question or chat in the middle of Church services but to wait and ask their husbands at home. The cultural context in which this instruction was given must also be considered. In Jewish churches, the women sat in one section, the men in another. Apparently the Corinthian women were not only chattering but also shouting questions to their husbands in the men's section. One person who works among Jewish people says that even today he has heard the president of a synagogue bang on the pulpit and shout to the women's section to be quiet. Proper order is Paul's concern in this passage and there is no conflict between this passage and his description of what a regular Church service should be:When ye come together, every one of you hath a psalm, hath a doctrine, hath a tongue, hath a revelation, hath an interpretation...If any man speak in an unknown tongue, let it be by two, or at the most by three...Let the prophets speak two or three...For ye may all prophesy one by one, that all may learn, and all may be comforted. (I Corinthians 14:26-27, 29, 31)

The pattern Paul describes for Church worship appears to be a very informal type of meeting. He tells every one that has a psalm, doctrine, tongue, revelation, or interpretation to present it in proper order. "Every one" includes women.

THE MORE SINFUL SEX?

In this passage Paul is not condemning women for their part in the fall into sin or indicating they are a more sinful sex. He is merely pointing out that when Eve acted in her own carnal will and authority she was deceived.

When you speak or act in a dictating, domineering spirit, you open yourself up to deception and sin.Paul is certainly not releasing man from his responsibility in the fall. Eve was deceived and thought she would become like a god. Adam was not deceived but sinned with full understanding of what he was doing and the consequences.

MARRIAGE

The believers in Corinth asked Paul about marriage and celibacy (remaining single for dedicated service unto the Lord). Paul's personal opinion was that the unmarried and widows were happier if they remained single:I say therefore to the unmarried and widows, it is good for them to abide even as I (that is, unmarried). (I Corinthians 7:8) He also commented:So then, he that giveth her in marriage doeth well; but he that giveth her not in marriage doeth better. (I Corinthians 7:38)

Paul stated in I Corinthians 7:2 that marriage provides for physical and emotional needs:Nevertheless, to avoid fornication, let every man have his own wife, and let every woman have her own husband. (I Corinthians 7:2)

Any single person, man or woman, who has a strong sexual desire should get married. Paul states his reason for suggesting people consider remaining single:...that ye may attend upon the Lord without distraction. (I Corinthians 7:35) Believers are only to marry other Christians. We are not to be "yoked together" with unbelievers in marriage.

WIDOWS

One passage in the Epistles refers to unmarried widows:Let not a widow be taken into the number (enrolled) under threescore years old, having been the wife of one man, well reported of for good works; if she have brought up children, if she have lodged strangers, if she have washed the saints' feet, if she have relieved the afflicted,

if she have diligently followed every good work. (I Timothy 5:9-10) A widow who wants to remain single and devote her life to ministry should be at least 60 years old, have been married only once, and have a good reputation for her Christian work.

Younger widows should not become members of this group because they might decide to marry again and break their vow to remain single for God's service. I Timothy 5 instructs the Church to provide for widows who have no family to provide for them.

WIVES

Marriage was ordained by God at the beginning of the world when He created Eve for Adam. God's original plan was one man for one woman for life. Divorce was not part of God's original plan but happened because of the "hardness" of man's heart. Sin-hardened hearts result in fornication, adultery, and desertion, all of which are Scriptural reasons for divorce.

Fornication is any kind of sexual immorality, for examples, homosexuality and incest. Adultery is having sexual relationships with someone who is not your mate. Paul explains:For the woman which hath an husband is bound by the law to her husband so long as he liveth; but if the husband be dead, she is loosed from the law of her husband.So then, if while her husband liveth, she be married to another man, she shall be called an adulteress; but if her husband be dead, she is free from that law; so that she is no adulteress, though she be married to another man. (Romans 7:2-3)

While these verses apply to the actual marriage relationship, they are also a type. Paul used this illustration to show how we must become dead to the law and its penalties in order to be married to Jesus Christ. No matter what sin we may have committed, when we come to Jesus the penalties imposed by Old Testament law are eliminated. We are no longer under, or married to, the law. Its hold over us is broken. We have a new relationship with Jesus Christ.

Even if you were divorced for unscriptural reasons, it is not the unpardonable sin. It can be forgiven by God just like any other sin. Marriage is honorable, but engaging in sexual relations outside of marriage is wrong: Marriage is honorable in all, and the bed undefiled; but whoremongers and adulterers God will judge. (Hebrews 13:4) Thessalonians records:For this is the will of God, even your sanctification, that ye should abstain from fornication. (I Thessalonians 4:3)Some general instructions are given in the Epistles regarding the wives of deacons in the Church:Even so must their wives be grave, not slanderers, sober, faithful in all things. (I Timothy 3:11)

Peter records a beautiful promise to wives who are married to unbelievers:Likewise, ye wives, be in subjection to your own husbands; that if, any obey not the word, they also may without the word be won by the conversation of the wives;While they behold your chaste conversation coupled with fear. (I Peter 3:1-2) Through loving submission, a woman with an unsaved husband can, without a word, lead him to God. The husband will observe the wife's holy conduct and her fear of God. He will notice the difference Christ makes in her life and through her example be drawn to the Savior.

Paul said if an unbelieving husband desires to remain with his wife, she is to stay with him:And the woman which hath an husband that believeth not, and if he be pleased to dwell with her, let her not leave him.But if the unbelieving depart, let him depart. A brother or sister is not under bondage in such cases. (I Corinthians 7:13 and 15)

The reason Paul gives for the wife to remain with an unbelieving husband:For what knoweth thou, O wife whether thou shalt save thy husband. (I Corinthians 7:16)In counseling, the question often arises as to whether a wife should stay with a husband who is physically abusing her and/or the children. If the abuse is sexual with the children, this is fornication and she has Scriptural grounds for divorce. But what about physical abuse...for example, beatings?

The Bible indicates that the body is the "temple of the Holy Ghost." It belongs to God, and whoever defiles this temple, the Lord will destroy him. When a woman remains with a husband who is physically abusing her and her children, she is setting that man up to be destroyed by God. She should remove herself and the children from his presence until he can be counseled and overcome this problem.

We have used several quotes from I Corinthians 7 to this point in this chapter. Pause now and read the entire chapter of I Corinthians which deals with the subject of singleness and marriage

CHAPTER TEN

THE RELATIONSHIP JESUS TO WOMEN

Introduction

It's true that Jesus choose twelve disciples which all of them were men, but from the beginning of Jesus ministry to the end, women were always around him working tirelessly. Jesus' high regard for women is seen in how He recognized their intrinsic equality with men, in how He ministered to women, and in the dignity, He accorded to women during his ministry.Jesus' recognition of role distinctions for men and women is demonstrated by His choosing only men to serve as His apostles with their primary tasks of preaching, teaching, and governing.

Women, however, served in other important capacities, such as praying, providing financial assistance, ministering to physical needs, voicing their theological understanding, and witnessing to the resurrection.Some may question whether Jesus' teaching and practice regarding the status of women harmonize with the rest of Biblical truth.

Was His teaching radically different from Old Testament revelation? Are Jesus and Paul contradictory? Is a wife's submission to her husband a one-way street, or are there mutual aspects involved in the teaching about submission? Different positions have been taken relative to these questions, ranging from that of radical feminists to more traditional evangelical views. The evangelical community seeks to interpret the text as inspired and authoritative. Such is the case with a number of evangelical feminists who are discarding the more traditional viewpoints.

WOMEN AND DISCIPLESHIP

Christ included women in His teaching. In Mark 7:10-11 He spoke of honoring parents, and repeated the words "father" and "mother" four times in two verses. There was a Greek word for "parents" which He could have used, but He apparently wanted to emphasize that both mother and father be honored equally.

When Jesus spoke regarding discipleship, He included the females:Suppose ye that I am come to give peace on earth? I tell you, Nay; but rather division.. The father shall be divided against the son, and the son against the father; the mother against the daughter, and the daughter against the mother; the mother-in-law against her daughter in law. (Luke 12:51,53)

Another passage regarding discipleship includes a reference to women:There is no man that hath left house, or brethren, or sisters, or father, or mother, or wife, or children ...for my sake and the gospel's, but he shall receive an hundred fold...houses, and brethren, and sisters, and mothers, and children. (Mark 10:29-30) On one occasion, when Jesus was speaking to a crowd, His mother and brothers came looking for Him.

When told they were seeking Him, Jesus said:Who is my mother? and who are my brethren? And he stretched forth his hand toward his disciples and said, Behold my mother and my brethren. For whosoever shall do the will of my Father...the same is my brother, and sister, and mother. (Matthew 12:46-50; Mark 3:31-35) This verse presents an important truth regarding your relationship to Jesus.

Your relationship is not based on whether you are male or female, young or old, married or single. Your relationship is based upon doing God's will. Part of "doing God's will" is accepting Jesus as personal Savior, as God is... ...not willing that any should perish, but that all should come to repentance. (II Peter 3:9)

WOMEN IN THE COMPANY OF CHRIST

Christ did not call a woman as one of the twelve disciples selected at the beginning of His public ministry. To have chosen a woman for such close association would not have been considered proper. The Bible does refer to certain women who joined the traveling company of Jesus to minister:It came to pass afterward, that he went throughout every city and village, preaching and shewing the glad tidings of the kingdom of God; and the twelve were with him.

And certain women, which had been healed of evil spirits and infirmities, Mary called Magdalene, out of whom went seven devils, And Joanna the wife of Chuza, Herod's steward, and Susanna, and many others, which ministered unto him of their substance. (Luke 8:1-3) Some people believe because Christ did not call any women among the original twelve, there should be no women leaders in the Church.

But He also did not choose a Gentile, yet the Gospel was extended to the Gentiles and we have had many great Gentile spiritual leaders. He did not organize anything resembling most Churches today, with one pastor trained in a seminary, Sunday schools, Church boards, etc., yet we freely use these in our Church structure.

DEFENSE OF WOMEN

On two occasions, Jesus defended women. When some mothers brought their children to Jesus to be blessed, the Disciples rebuked them but Jesus said: Suffer the little children to come unto me, and forbid them not; for of such is the Kingdom of God. (Mark 10:14)When Mary of Bethany poured costly perfume on Jesus, the Disciples called it a waste. Jesus said her act would be told as a memorial wherever the Gospel was preached because she understood the plan for His death and burial and was anointing Him in preparation forit.

CHAPTER ELEVEN

MINISTRY TO WOMEN

Introduction As you studied this book however, you may have felt a special call to minister to women. This chapter provides guidelines on how to start a ministry to women. It includes suggestions for organizing and advertising your group and instructions on identifying women's unique spiritual needs.

HOW TO START A MINISTRY TO WOMEN

• Begin to pray for direction from God and for the women of your area.

• Call together a small group of Christian women to assist in organizing the ministry. Seek out those whose hearts God has touched with similar spiritual vision and purpose. Begin to pray together for women in your community.

• During these prayer sessions ask the Lord to help you identify the purpose for your womens' ministry. Your "statement of purpose" should answer the questions "Why do we exist? What is it God wants us to accomplish through us?"It is important to determine this purpose because the

Bible indicates, "Where there is no vision, the people perish." Just as individuals need a purpose for living, a group needs a purpose for existence. There are many different purposes for which a women's ministry may be established. A group may have one or several of the following purposes:

• Prayer: You can meet together to pray for your community, your nation, your leaders, and the world. Through prayer you can effectively penetrate every region of the world and become the undergirding force behind those on the forefront of evangelism.

• Bible study: The purpose of your group may be to study God's Word together with the goal of leading women to spiritual maturity.

• Evangelism: Your purpose may be to reach your community, city, or village with the Gospel through various evangelical outreaches.Ministry to younger women: You may adopt the Biblical principle of the older Christian women teaching the younger. If so, your statement of purpose is already written for you in Titus 2:3-4

• Special group ministry: You may minister to special groups of women, i.e., unwed mothers, women on drugs, alcoholics, prison inmates, children, juvenile delinquents, women on college campuses in your city, or women in rest homes and hospitals.

You may feel called to minister to women in certain geographical areas or depressed regions, i.e., in economically deprived areas.Special group ministries provide unlimited possibilities of purpose for a women's group. Analyze your area. What spiritually needy groups are not being reached? This may be the special challenge God has for you.

• Church auxiliary: You may organize a women's group as an auxiliary of your church. Your purpose would be to provide support for the various programs of the church.

• Missionary auxiliary: The purpose of this group would be to provide prayer financial, and material assistance to missionaries.

• World Christians: The purpose of this group would be to focus attention, prayer, and action on the global cause of reaching the world with the Gospel of Jesus Christ.

• STEP FIVE:Advertise your womens' group to let women of your community know about the date, time, place, and purpose of your meetings. Whether your advertising plan is as simple as word of mouth in a village or a complex advertising campaign in the city, you must get the message out. As the New Testament commands, "Go out in the highways and byways, and compel them to come in."

The following are suggestions for advertising your group. The ideas you use will depend on your geographic location and the funds available for advertising:

1. Obtain permission from your pastor to post notices on the church bulletin board and in the adult Sunday School classrooms.

2. Ask the pastor to announce the meeting from the pulpit the Sunday immediately prior to each meeting.

3 . Ask your pastor to print a notice in the church bulletin if your church publishes one .

4. Take a supply of posters to your local Christian bookstore. Ask the owner to put one on the bulletin board and stack a supply on the counter .

5. If your city has a Chamber of Commerce, ask if they will give a printed announcement (which you will supply)

to new residents who stop by to pick up information on the community.

6. Give flyers to women in your neighborhood, church, women's organizations, and at your job.

7. Leave supplies of flyers in Laundromats, markets, and beauty shops...anywhere women frequent. (Be sure to obtain permission of the store management).

8. The public library may have a place for local announcements. If so, keep it supplied.

9. Send a letter of invitation to:-Wives of pastors.-Lists of names obtained from local women.-Leaders of secular women's groups.-Lists of women obtained from local churches and denomination.

10. Announce your meetings on radio, television, and in the newspaper, if your area has these available.

• STEP SIX:You are now ready to begin meeting as a womens' group. Here are some suggestions for...The First Meeting:

1. Obtain the name and address of each person in attendance. This will enable you to contact these women for future meetings.

2. Prior to the meeting, prepare copies of the information on the name and purpose of your group. Distribute and review these during the first meeting.

3. Discuss the plans you have for your group: For example, opportunities for ministry, fellowship, training, etc. Women must recognize the personal spiritual benefits of involvement and be challenged by the plans of the local chapter

4. Provide opportunity for praise and worship, ministry from the Word of God, and prayer for needs of those in attendance. The ministry portion of this first meeting is

very important. If women have their spiritual needs met and learn more about God and His Word, they will return for future meetings .

5. Provide flyers or posters to those in attendance along with instructions for telling others about your group. Encourage them to use these materials to invite others to the meetings

• .Following Meetings:Here are suggestions for future meetings:

1. Always welcome and register visitors. Provide them with a copy of the information on the name and purpose of your group.

2. Provide opportunity for praise and worship, ministry from the Word of God, and prayer for needs.

• STEP SEVEN: Contact all those who attended the first meeting with either a card, telephone call, or visit prior to the next meeting. This practice should be maintained for all visitors present in future meetings. Encourage them to return and become a regular part of your group

A CHALLENGE FOR DEDICATION: To rise up and take our rightful position as Godly women requires dedication. Paul presents a challenge to all believers including women.

It is a call to dedication: I appeal to you..to make a decisive dedication of your bodies-presenting all your members and faculties-as a living sacrifice, holy, devoted, consecrated and well pleasing to God which is your reasonable, rational, intelligent service and spiritual worship. Do not be conformed to this world-this age, fashioned after and adapted to itsexternal, superficial customs.

But be transformed, changed by the entire renewal of your mind, by its new ideals and its new attitude. So that you may prove what is the good and acceptable and perfect will of God, even the thing which is good and acceptable and perfect in His sight for you. (Romans 12:1-2) Dedication to God and discipline to the ways of God results in direction which leads to knowledge of the perfect will of God in your life.

CHAPTER TWELVE

ROLE OF THE WOMEN IN CHURCH

Having dealt with the negatives we will now look at the positives. What are women to do in the churches? In no sense is it a limited role. There is plenty to keep everyone busy.

Good works

In his first letter to Timothy the Apostle speaks of some needy old women who were to receive preferential treatment by the church. Where widows had children, the family were to look after them, but if they were on their own, widows indeed, they were to be looked after by the church and in return would give themselves to supplications and prayers. Only the very best were to be chosen for this special position. It is worth noting the distinguishing characteristics of these godly women. One is, 'Well reported of for good works ... if she have diligently followed every good work' (1 Tim. 5:10). All of us will one day be judged according to our works (Rev. 20:13). Good works are kind deeds and they show that our faith is real. There is huge scope here for all women and of course for men too.

Bringing up children

One of the features of these specially-godly women is, 'if she have brought up children' (1 Tim. 5:10). This is something not particularly valued today. When children are born the question is soon asked of the young mother, 'When are you going back to work?' The all-important thing is to earn money and progress in one's career. Yet, in the eyes of God, the caring for, and training of covenant children is of immense value. When we die, money and careers will be left behind but if we have brought up children for the Lord that will be something of value to all eternity. Not all women, of course, are given husbands and not all couples are given children, but where they are, they have something to do of immense value and eternal significance. Mothers are the main influence on young children and many of us thank God for our mothers and the mighty influence they were upon us under the hand of God. Even in secular terms, as the poet said, 'He that rocks the cradle rules the world'; how much more in spiritual terms?

Hospitality

A further point made by the Apostle here is, 'if she have lodged strangers' (1 Tim. 5:10). No man was to be appointed as an elder but such as was 'given to hospitality' (1 Tim. 3:2). Lydia's conversion was evidenced by the fact that 'she besought us, saying, if ye have judged me to be faithful to the Lord, come into my house, and abide there. And she constrained us' (Acts 16:15). John writes to 'the elect lady and her children' (2 Jn. 1). She was used to accommodating preachers but she must not receive heretics (v 10). Hospitality is an expression of Christian love.

Washing the saints' feet

Those women who were to be 'taken into the number' were such as had 'washed the saints' feet' (1 Tim. 5:10). Jesus washed the disciples' feet and said, 'If I then, your Lord and Master, have washed your feet; ye also ought to wash one another's feet. For I have given you an example, that ye should do as I have done to you' (Jn. 13:14-15). Should we practise foot-washing? The pope, each year, ostentatiously washes the feet of some beggars in Rome. If one lived in the hot, dusty, Middle East, wore sandals and spent the day walking the roads, then the washing of one's feet would be a welcome relief on entering a home. However what we have here is a pattern not a precept. It calls us to acts of humble service done in kindness to others for their refreshment and comfort. The lowest servant in the house washed the feet and the godly should happily take that lowest position for the comfort of others.

Relieve the afflicted

Often when thinking of the role of women the emphasis is placed upon doing high-profile, self-exalting work. However, we see that the Scripture rather lays emphasis upon service. Jesus said, 'If any man (or woman) desire to be first, the same shall be last of all, and servant of all' (Mk. 9:35). Paul commends to Timothy the women who have 'relieved the afflicted' (1 Tim. 5:10).This would entail visiting the sick or any who are needy, giving them time, providing support, comfort, medicines and food.

Supplications and Prayers

The kind of widow of whom the Apostle speaks here, 'trusteth in God, and continueth in supplications and prayers night and day' (1 Tim. 5:5). Few can estimate the value of the earnest prayers of godly women. Many congregations would be in a poor state but for this dedicated ministry carried out by godly women unnoticed by the world. Prayer is mighty because God is all-powerful and loves to answer the cries of His own.

Caring for ageing relatives

Much of the greatest work that we can do for God attracts little praise from man, but is a sweet savour, a beautiful deed, a delightful perfume to God. The Bible says, 'But if any provide not for his own, and specially for those of his own house, he hath denied the faith, and is worse than an infidel' (1 Tim. 5:8). Where widows had children the family were duty-bound to support them; 'let them relieve them, and let not the church be charged; that it may relieve them that are widows indeed' (v 16). In our day it is easy to place ageing relatives in a nursing home. Sometimes that is necessary because of the constant care (24/7) the loved one requires, but the ideal is for Christians to provide such care for their own. This is God-glorifying. As someone said, 'A poor parent can bring up ten children but ten rich children cannot care for one old parent'.

Listening to Jesus

Moving away from 1 Timothy 5 there is much teaching in the rest of Scripture. Martha and Mary entertained Jesus in their home. Martha felt the strain of having to provide a meal for so many and was angry with her sister for not helping more. She came to Jesus to complain: 'Lord, dost thou not care that my sister hath left me to serve alone? bid her therefore that she help me'. But we notice Jesus' surprising answer, 'Martha, Martha, thou art careful and troubled about many things: But one thing is needful: and Mary hath chosen that good part, which shall not be taken away from her' (Lk. 10:40-42). Women are to choose the good part, studying the Word of God, listening to sermons and reading good books. In this way they will build up their theological knowledge and feed their faith and that of others.

Evangelism

One of the most effective evangelists in the Scripture was a woman, and a despised, sinful, Samaritan woman at that. When she found salvation herself she went to the people of her town and shouted, 'Come, see a man, which told me all things that ever I did: is not this the Christ? Then they went out of the city, and came unto him' (Jn. 4:29-30). Many of the people of her town believed in Jesus because of her words and others believed when they heard Him for themselves. How many people are saved today through women who gossip the gospel to their friends and neighbours?

Witnesses of the Resurrection

In a day when women were generally despised it is worth noticing that the very first witness to whom Christ appeared after His resurrection was a woman (Jn. 20:15-17). Mary Magdalene then went and told the disciples what she had seen and heard. She proclaimed the risen Christ to the future leaders of the church. Why did He first appear to her? No doubt because of her great love, her presence at the cross till He died, her being first at the grave on the resurrection morning, but also so that all women would be encouraged to bear testimony to the risen Christ.

Teaching the younger women

Paul writes to Titus with regard to the older ladies, 'That they be in behaviour as becometh holiness, not false accusers, not given to much wine, teachers of good things; that they may teach the young women to be sober, to love their husbands, to love their children, to be discreet, chaste, keepers at home, good, obedient to their own husbands, that the word of God be not blasphemed' (Tit. 2:3-5). More mature women are to teach the younger ones and to be an example to them. 'Keepers at home' means keepers of the home and home-makers, a very important role for women. A home without a mother usually loses that which holds it together. Also, it is implied that as an extension of the home, women can teach the children of others, for example in a sabbath school.

Informal teaching of men

Women, as we noticed, are forbidden to preach or perform public teaching. However it is fascinating to notice how Priscilla was involved in informal and private teaching of a man. Apollos had arrived in Ephesus and preached in the synagogue with great eloquence and demonstrated a very considerable knowledge of the Scriptures, but he knew only the baptism of John. The book of Acts tells us, 'And he began to speak boldly in the synagogue: whom when Aquila and Priscilla had heard, they took him unto them, and expounded unto him the way of God more perfectly' (Acts 18:26). It was not simply Aquila who taught him but it is specially mentioned that Priscilla was involved. Perhaps she was the more gifted and theologically astute of the two. It could be argued that while husband and wife are mentioned together, it was actually Aquila who did the 'expounding'? But then why is her name given and not just here? Indeed in Romans 16:3 her name is given before her husband. Most other Christian workers would also have wives but they are not mentioned. Obviously she performed a very significant role in correcting the theology of Apollos. Women have a duty to share their knowledge of the Scriptures and of theology in an informal way and many a woman has been a great blessing in a private way and also in informal gatherings.

Conclusion

The Old Testament gives an account of many faithful and godly women who were very influential: Sarah, Rebekah, Deborah, Ruth, Hannah, Abigail, Huldah and Esther, to mention a few. Similarly in the New Testament we have Mary the mother of Jesus, Elisabeth, Anna, Mary Magdalene, Mary of Bethany, Dorcas, Phebe, Tryphena and Tryphosa, Euodias and Syntyche and many more who laboured in the gospel and whose work was greatly appreciated by Paul and the early church.

Following his clear instruction that women are not to be public preachers the Apostle says, 'Notwithstanding she shall be saved in childbearing, if they continue in faith and charity and holiness with sobriety' (1 Tim.2:15). Many strange views are given of this verse. The simplest and most biblical way to understand it is that salvation comes through women in the sense that one bears the child, Jesus, through whom salvation comes to mankind. Although sin entered through a woman, deliverance also comes through a woman, Mary. Praise God for godly women!

CHAPTER THIRTEEN

ALL WOMEN LIST IN THE OT & NT

<u>Old Testament Women in the New Testament</u>

 Tamar (Matt. 1:3)

 Rahab (Matt 1:5; Heb 11:31; James 2:25)

 Ruth (Matt. 1:5)

 Bathsheba (Matt. 1:6)

 Rachel (2:18)

 The Queen of the South (Matt 12:42; Luke 11:31)

 Widows in Israel (Luke 4:25)

 Widow of Zarephath (Luke 4:25-26)

 Wives who were destroyed by the flood (Luke 17:27)

 Lot's wife (Luke 17:32)

 Sara (Rom, 4:19; 9:9; Gal 4:22-31; Heb 11:11; 1 Pet. 3:6)

 Rebecca (Rom 9:10-12)

 Eve (2 Cor. 11:3)

 Hagar (Gal 4:22-31)

 Jezebel and her children (Rev 2:20-23)

 Pharaoh's daughter (Acts 7:21; Heb 11:24-26)

Moses' parents (Heb 11:23)

Holy women (1 Peter 3:5)

Women received their dead to life (Heb 11:35-36).

All the Women in the New Testament

Mary (Matt 1:16, 18-25; 2-11, 13-14, 20-21; Matt 12:46-50; Matt 13:55; Mark 3: 31-35; Mark 6:3; Luke 1:26-56; 2:5-8, 16, 19, 22, 27, 34-35, 43-51; Luke 8: 19-20; John 2:1-5, 12; 6:42; John 19:25-27; Acts 1:14; Gal 4:4)

Peter's Mother-in-law (Matt 8:14-15; Mark 1:30-31; Luke 4:38-39)

Daughter of Jarius (Matt 9: 18-19, 23-26; Mark 5: 22-24, 35-43; Luke 8:41, 49-56)

Wife of Jarius (Mark 5:40-43; Luke 8:51-56)

Woman with Issue of Blood (Matt 9: 20-22; Mark 5:25-34; Luke 8:43-48)

Christ's Sisters (Matt 13:56; Mark 6:3)

Herodias (Matt. 14: 1-11; Mark 6:17-28; Luke 3:19-20)

Herodias' daughter (Matt 14:6-11; Mark: 6: 22-29; Luke 3:19-20)

Women and children among the 5,000 (Matt 14:21)

Women and children among the 4,000 (Matt 15:38)

Syrophenician woman (also called the Woman of Canaan) (Matt 15:21-28, Mark 7:24-30)

Young daughter of the Syrophenician woman (Matt 15:21-28, Mark 7:24-30)

The Mother of Zebedee's Children (Matt 20:20-23; Matt 27:56)

Woman who Anointed Jesus (Matt 26: 6-13; Mark 14:3-9; John 12:1-8)

Damsel to whom Peter denied Christ (Matt 26:69; Mark 14:66- 68; John 18: 17)

Maid to whom Peter denied Christ (Matt 26:71: Mark 14: 69-70; Luke 22:56-57)

Wife of Pontius Pilate (Matt 27:19)

Many women beholding a far off (Matt 27:55-56; mark 15: 40-41)

Mary Magdalene (Matt 27:57, 61; Matt 28:1-10; Mark 15: 40-41,47; 16: 1-8, 9-11; Luke 8:2-3; 24: 1-11, 22-24; John 19:25; 20: 1-3, 11-18)

Mary, the mother of James and Joses (also called "The other Mary") (Matt 27:56, 61; 28:1-10; Mark 15: 40-41,47; 16: 1-8; Luke 24: 1-11, 22-24)

The Widow who Gave Two Mites (Mark 12:41-44; Luke 21:1-4)

Salome (Mark 15: 40-41; Mark 16: 1-8)

Many other woman which came up with Jesus from Galilee (Mark 15: 40-41)

Elisabeth (Luke 1:5-80)

Anna (Luke 2: 36-38)

Widow of Nain (Luke 7: 11-17)

Sinner who washed Jesus Feet with her hair (Luke 7:36-50)

Certain women who had been healed (Luke 8:2-3)

Joanna, the wife of Chuza (Luke 8:2-3; Luke 24: 1-11, 22-24)

Susana (Luke 8:2-3)

Martha (Luke 10: 37-42; John 11: 1-6, 17-27, 34-45; 12:2)

Mary of Bethany (Luke 10: 37-42; John 11: 1-5, 17-20, 28-34, 39-45; 12:3-9)

Certain woman of the company (Luke 11:27-28)

Woman with a Spirit of Infirmity (Luke 13:11-16)

Women which bewailed and lamented (Luke 23: 27-29)

Women that followed Jesus (Luke 23: 49, 55-56)

Other women at the empty tomb (Luke 24: 1-11, 22-24)

Samaritan Woman at the Well (John 4: 7-42)

Woman Taken in Adultery (John 8:1-11)

The mother of the Man Born Blind (John 9:2-3, 18-23)

Mary, the wife of Cleophas (John 19:25)

His Mother's sister (John 19:25)

Apostles gathered in Prayer and Supplication with the Women (Acts 1:14)

Sapphira (Acts 5:1-11)

New Women Believers (Acts 5: 14)

Widows who were neglected (Acts 6:1)

Women committed to prison by Paul (Acts 8:3; Acts 22:4)

Samaritan women baptized by Philip (Acts 8:12)

Candance, queen of Ethiopians (Acts 8:27)

Women Persecuted by Paul bring them bound (Acts 9:2)

Tabitha/Dorcus (Acts 9:36-42)

Mary, the Mother of John Mark (Acts 12:12; Col 4:10)

Rhoda (Acts 12:13-15)

Devout and Honorable Jewish Women (Acts 13:50)

Eunice (2 Tim 1:15; Acts 16:1—the son of a certain woman)

Lois (2 Tim 1:15)

Women at the Place of Prayer in Philippi (Acts 16:13)

Lydia (Acts 16: 11-15, 40)

Certain Damsel Possessed with a Spirit of Divination (Acts 16:16-19)

Chief and Honorable Women of the Greeks (Acts 17:4, 12)

Damris (Acts 17:34)

Priscilla (Acts 18:2-3, 18-20, 24-26; Rom. 16: 3-5; 1 Cor. 16:19; 2 Tim 4:19)

Wives and children of Tyre (Acts 21:4-6)

Four Daughters of Philip (Acts 21:9)

Paul's sister (Acts 23:16)

Drusilla (Acts 24:24)

Bernice (Acts 25:13-14, 23; 26:30)

Phebe (Romans 16:1-2)

Mary of Rome (Rom. 16:6)

Junia (Rom. 16: 7)

Tryphena (Roman 16:12)

Tryphosa (Rom 16:12)

Persis (Rom. 16:12

Mother of Rufus (Rom. 16: 13)

Sister of Nerus (Rom. 16: 15)

Julia (Rom. 16:15)

Chloe (1 Corinthians 1:11)

Euodia (Phillip 4: 2-3) — she is called Euodias in the KJV (a male name) but it is possible she was female

Syntyche (Phillip 4:2-3)

Claudia (2 Tim 4:21)

Ye adulterers and adulteresses (James 4:4)

Apphia (Philemon 1:2)

The Elect Lady (2 John)

The Elect Lady's Sister (2 John 1:13)

Nympha (Colossians 4:15) — called Nymphas in KJV but is possibly female.

Sources

Bauckham, Richard Gospel Women. Chicago: T&T Clark, 2002.

Borland, James A. "Women in the Life and Teachings of Jesus" Faculty Publications and Presentations. Paper 110. 1991.

Brown, Raymond E. "Roles of Women in the Fourth Gospel, theological Studies 36. 1975. James, Carolyn Custis Lost Women of the Bible. Zondervan, 2005.

Jewett, Paul K. Man as Male and Female.

Spencer, Aida Bensançon "Women in the Church: A Biblical Study of the Role of Women in the Church", Trinity Journal 8:1 Spring, 1987

Spencer, Aída Besançon 'Jesus' Treatment of Women in the Gospels' in RW Pierce and RM Groothuis (eds) Discovering Biblical Equality. IVP, 2005

Edwards, Ruth B The Case for Women's Ministry. SPCK, 1989.

Evans, Mary J. Women in the Bible: An Overview of All the Crucial Passages on Women's Roles. Downers Grove, IL: InterVarsity Press, 1983.

Freebies, Scripture StudyBy Heather FarrellMay 29, 2014

www.ingramcontent.com/pod-product-compliance
Lightning Source LLC
Chambersburg PA
CBHW051244160726
47994CB00003B/1017